MOVIE MONSTERS

MOVIE MONSTERS

David Baird

MQP

INTRODUCTION

From the moment mankind discovered we were able to capture images on film and make them dance about on the big screen, the notion of using this new medium to scare the living daylights out of audiences—as a form of entertainment—immediately sprang to mind. Among the first to explore the possibilities of a medium capable of simultaneously attracting and repelling us, was pioneer filmmaker Georges Méliès. In 1896, he made a horror movie that was just over three minutes long entitled *Le Manoir du Diable (The Devil's Castle)*, which contained several motifs that would be explored in a number of later vampire films.

The sudden explosion in both the technical possibilities and popularity of the cinema in the twentieth century saw filmmakers frantically delving through folklore, legends, ghost stories, spooky fables, and, of course, great novels by the likes of Bram Stoker, Mary Shelley, and Gaston Leroux. They were searching for legendary monsters who would send shivers down the lengths of our spines for generations to come—and they found them in Dracula, Frankenstein's monster, the Mummy, and countless others.

It is impossible to think of Frankenstein's monster without envisaging the actor Boris Karloff or to mention Dracula without immediately recalling the haunting voice and intense close-ups of Bela Lugosi. The great Christopher Lee, who played every chilling character imaginable, gave us many a sleepless night and between the two masters of disguise, Lon Cheney and Lon Cheney Junior, we were presented with a frighteningly realistic Phantom of the Opera, Wolf Man, and Hunchback of Notre Dame, to name but a few.

Whatever form the monsters may take—from giant apes discovered on fog-shrouded islands to subterranean serpents that surface to feed, from creatures created in the laboratories of mad scientists to robots or aliens from distant planets, and not forgetting ghosts, spirits, and monstrous humans possessed by evil—one thing is certain, we all love to fear them!

Cinema may not have survived without these grotesque creatures and terrifying beasts. From very modest beginnings, screen monsters have evolved through state-of-the-art techniques and computer-generated imagery into the almost unimaginable beings of modern movies, which are capable of unleashing the terror that lurks within each of us.

Movie Monsters seeks to celebrate the many astonishing and unforgettable creatures we all love to fear. Of course, we all have our favorites. If yours has been neglected, then let the experience of reading this book help to bring back to mind the vivid memories of just what it was that made it so monstrous. The next time you are out walking and see a sinister group of birds congregating on the telephone wires or hear a spine-chilling howl in the distance just remember this…they were only movies!

PRESIDENT DALE: Why can't we work out our differences? Why can't we work things out? Little people, why can't we all just get along?

 MARS ATTACKS!
Dir. Tim Burton (1996)

FILM FACT: Director Tim Burton was apparently told over and over again that under no circumstances must he kill off Jack Nicholson's character in a movie…any movie. Rising to the challenge, Burton cast Nicholson in two different roles in the movie—and both characters were killed by the aliens!

QUASIMODO: I'm about as shapeless as the man in the moon!

 HUNCHBACK OF NOTRE DAME
Dir. William Dieterle (1939)

FILM FACT: Actor Charles Laughton played some wonderfully memorable roles during his career but perhaps most notable was his portrayal of Quasimodo, the lovelorn Parisian hunchback. It took almost three hours a day to fully apply his gruesome makeup and because no pictures of him in full costume and makeup were allowed to be seen in advance, each and every member of the viewing audience was guaranteed the shock of seeing it for the first time on the big screen.

In space no one can hear you scream.

Tagline from the film

ALIEN
Dir. Ridley Scott (1979)

FILM FACT: There have been all sorts of rumors and intrigues surrounding the making of *Alien*, but the most infamous is the fact that none of the cast, apart from John Hurt, knew exactly what to expect while filming the moment when the Alien literally "bursts" onto the scene. That is why the expressions on the cast's blood-splattered faces look so authentic!

STEPHEN BANNING: It is the mummy that lives…the mummy I brought to life when I read the scroll. It hates us for desecrating the tomb of its princess! It will kill us! All of us!

THE MUMMY
Dir. Terence Fisher (1959)

FILM FACT: Bandages must have seemed quite appropriate for Christopher Lee, who played the mighty Mummy awakened by a trio of unfortunate archeologists. During shooting he suffered a catalog of bruises, bangs, burns, and bumps. Most notably—and painfully—Lee dislocated his shoulder when he crashed into a door, which, instead of breaking away as planned, held firm because an overzealous stagehand had securely bolted it closed!

BATMAN: I'm going to kill you!
JOKER: You idiot! You made me.
Remember, you dropped me into
that vat of chemicals. That wasn't
easy to get over, and don't think
that I didn't try.

BATMAN
Dir. Tim Burton (1989)

FILM FACT: As much mystery surrounded the
casting of this film as surrounds the caped
crusader himself. The producers wanted Jack
Nicholson to play the Joker, but he wasn't biting.
So, they made him believe that another star
wanted the part—and he suddenly said yes!
Whether fact or fable, the casting was inspired and
Nicholson got the last laugh through a lucrative
deal giving him a royalty on all merchandise and a
percentage of the box office takings.

Created in a weird scientist's laboratory…from the skeletons of two women and the heart of a living girl!

Tagline from the film

BRIDE OF FRANKENSTEIN
Dir. James Whale (1935)

FILM FACT: Elsa Lanchester, who played the monster's bride, wasn't very tall so she spent the entire film trussed to stilts to make her seven feet tall. Strangely, her supporting cast (no pun intended!) were even more unlucky with their legs. Colin Clive (Dr. Frankenstein), broke his leg in a horse riding accident shortly before filming began and spent most of the movie seated and Boris Karloff (the monster) fell into a well during filming and emerged with a broken leg.

> But first, on earth as Vampire sent,
> Thy corpse shall from the tomb be rent:
> Then ghastly haunt thy native place,
> And suck the blood of all thy race;

Lord Byron

 NOSFERATU, EINE SYMPHONIE DES GRAUENS (NOSFERATU, A SYMPHONY OF HORRORS)
Dir. F. W. Manau (1922)

FILM FACT: It is over eighty years old, yet Max Schreck's vampire performance is still the most hauntingly beautiful and atmospheric portrayal ever created, despite being shot without the permission of Bram Stoker, writer of *Dracula*. Stoker's widow took legal action against the film company concerned and all known prints and negatives had to be destroyed. Fortunately for modern audiences, a few copies survived and the movie is now widely available.

WICKED WITCH OF THE WEST: Take your army to the Haunted Forest and bring me that girl and her dog.... Take special care of those ruby slippers. I want those most of all. Now fly, fly!

THE WIZARD OF OZ
Dir. Victor Fleming (1939)

FILM FACT: Margaret Hamilton, who played the Wicked Witch of the West, had her fair share of accidents during filming. She was badly burned when her cape got caught in the burst of fire that appeared when she vanished from Munchkinland. Her terrifying winged-monkey henchmen weren't quite so unfortunate, but it is interesting to note that their leader was called Nikko, which is the name of a small town in Japan famous for its sculpture of the "hear no evil, see no evil, speak no evil" monkeys.

ANNIE WILKES: I am your number one fan. There is nothing to worry about. You are going to be just fine. I am your number one fan.

MISERY
Dir. Rob Reiner (1990)

FILM FACT: Screenwriter William Goldman was so stirred by the horrendous moment in Stephen King's novel *Misery* in which Annie Wilkes cuts off writer Paul Sheldon's feet that he decided to adapt the book for the big screen. However, the script was revised shortly before filming to have Annie breaking Paul's ankles with a sledgehammer instead. Once Goldman saw the scene captured so effectively and appallingly on screen he was happy for the change to be kept.

The epic story that was destined to stand as a colossus of adventure!

Tagline from the film

JASON AND THE ARGONAUTS
Dir. Don Chaffey (1963)

FILM FACT: This wonderful epic used the special effects skills of Ray Harryhausen to the full—the truly thrilling three-minute scene of Jason battling an army of sword-wielding skeletons took him more than four months to produce because he could only create thirteen frames of film a day! Filming was also delayed off the coast of Italy when, midway through shooting a sailing scene, a fine replica of the ship the *Golden Hind* from the television series *Sir Francis Drake* sailed into view—losing both film crews their shots.

MITCH BRENNER: I think we're in real trouble…. The bird war, the bird attack, plague, call it what you like. They're amassing out there someplace and they'll be back. You can count on it…

 ## THE BIRDS
Dir. Alfred Hitchcock (1963)

FILM FACT: It took several days to shoot the scenes in which the birds ravage Tippi Hedren's character Melanie, and the actress found it quite an ordeal: "on the last day, one of [the birds] jumped from my shoulder and really cut me, way too close to the eye. And I got the birds off and just sat in the middle of the set crying…" Hitchcock needed to find a way to stop the birds from flying away, so the crew came up with the idea of attaching them to the actress's clothes using long invisible nylon threads.

THE INVISIBLE MAN: An invisible man can rule the world. No one will see him come; no one will see him go. He can rob, and rape, and kill!

 ## THE INVISIBLE MAN
Dir. James Whale (1933)

FILM FACT: Director James Whale only ever had one actor in mind to play the scientist-turned-villain of H. G. Wells's classic novel *The Invisible Man*—Claude Rains. Whale felt that the actor's distinctive, sophisticated, and intelligent voice made him perfect for the role and he wouldn't even consider the studio's choice, Boris Karloff, who was famous for playing the monsters in *Frankenstein* and *The Mummy*.

That child of Hell had
nothing human; nothing lived
in him but fear and hatred…

Robert Louis Stevenson

 THE OMEN
Dir. Richard Donner (1976)

FILM FACT: Are you at all superstitious? You would be if you were involved in
the making of *The Omen*. The film seemed to have been cursed from the
outset. The screenwriter's plane was struck by lightning, the director's hotel
was bombed, star Gregory Peck narrowly missed being a passenger on an
airplane that crashed leaving no survivors, and on the first day of shooting,
several members of the crew were involved in a serious car crash.

Mighty panorama of Earth-shaking fury as an army from Mars invades!

Tagline from the film

 ## THE WAR OF THE WORLDS
Dir. Byron Haskin (1953)

FILM FACT: Many people truly believed aliens were invading the earth after listening to Orson Welles's notorious *The War of the Worlds* radio broadcast in 1938, so it is little wonder that he rejected the offer to direct this film version of H. G. Wells's science fiction classic. Byron Haskin took on the responsibility of directing instead, spending an, at that time, massive $1,400,000 on special effects to bring to life the Martian machine models, which were apparently based on the shape and movements of swans.

ROY BATTY: I've seen things you people wouldn't believe. Attack ships on fire off the shoulder of Orion. I watched C-beams glitter in the dark near the Tannhauser gate. All those moments will be lost in time, like tears in rain. Time to die.

BLADE RUNNER
Dir. Ridley Scott (1982)

FILM FACT: Rick Deckard is a cop-like "Blade Runner" played by Harrison Ford who specializes in terminating human clones called replicants. Ford had it straight from director Ridley Scott that Deckard was human and not a replicant himself, so that is how the star brilliantly played the part. However, when pressed on the subject eighteen years later, Ridley Scott declared that Deckard was in fact a replicant. This may have thrown Harrison Ford, but perhaps goes some way to explaining why, in one scene, a red glow is seen in Deckar's eyes, a telltale sign that someone isn't what they appear to be...

MALEVA: Whoever is bitten by a werewolf and lives becomes a werewolf himself.

THE WOLF MAN
Dir. George Waggner (1941)

FILM FACT: Although most people believe it is a traditional saying, screenwriter Curt Siodmak admitted to making up the famous line, "Even a man who is pure at heart, and says his prayers by night, may become a wolf when the wolfbane blooms and the autumn moon is bright" for this movie. It has appeared in almost every werewolf film since and is now an integral part of werewolf mythology.

COLONEL ARMROUGE: Our job is to prevent a possible nation-wide panic by keeping the information from the public.

INVASION OF THE SAUCER MEN
Dir. Edward L. Cahn (1957)

FILM FACT: *Invasion of the Saucer Men* may not have won any Academy Awards, but it has become quite popular with teenagers over the years. You can't help wondering if the movie may have earned its cult status because of the wicked aliens' novel method of killing the earthlings—injecting alcohol into the bloodstream of their victims. Something many teenagers would no doubt know all about!

He who fights with monsters might take care lest he thereby become a monster. And if you gaze for long into an abyss, the abyss gazes also into you.

Friedrich Nietzsche

THE SILENCE OF THE LAMBS
Dir. Jonathan Demme (1991)

FILM FACT: It is odd to think that Gene Hackman, Robert Duvall, or even Jeremy Irons might have played Dr. Hannibal Lecter, the role Anthony Hopkins so successfully made his own. Even more so if you close your eyes and listen to him delivering his most famous cannabalistic line—in a voice he said was "a combination of Truman Capote and Katherine Hepburn"—accompanied by his unforgettable slurping hiss. Hopkins delivers such a memorable 16 minutes of screen time that it's no wonder he won an Oscar.

Don't get him wet, keep him out of bright light, and never feed him after midnight.

Tagline from the film

GREMLINS 2: THE NEW BATCH
Dir. Joe Dante (1990)

FILM FACT: *Gremlins 2* is packed with immediately recognizable references and tributes to other films, ranging from *Batman* to *The Wizard of Oz*, but perhaps its best spoof is of an "end of the world" video. Director Joe Dante simply had to include his own hilarious version in *Gremlins 2* after he discovered that at least one television news network already had such a tape prepared...just in case!

Put yourself in her place!
The dreaded night when
her lover became a madman.

Tagline from the film

DR. JEKYLL AND MR. HYDE
Dir. Rouben Mamoulian (1931)

FILM FACT: Long before today's computer-generated imagery (CGI) produced such special effects, this movie proved it was way ahead of its time when it showed the most amazing onscreen transformation. A series of filters were placed before the camera lens masking different parts of actor Frederic March's makeup and then removed in sequence—transforming him from the moralistic Dr. Jekyll into the terrifying Mr. Hyde.

45

MAX CADY: I understand, I'm not your type, too many tattoos. Thing is, there isn't much to do in prison except desecrate your flesh.

 CAPE FEAR
Dir. Martin Scorsese (1991)

FILM FACT: Not one to shy away from getting into a role, Robert De Niro had his body tattooed using vegetable dyes and paid a dentist an alleged $5,000 to make his teeth look bad for the part of the monster, Max Cady. After filming finished, he had to pay the dentist four times as much to get them looking good again.

47

MRS. MILLS: Sometimes the world of the living gets mixed up with the world of the dead.

THE OTHERS
Dir. Alejandro Amenábar (2001)

FILM FACT: Spanish filmmaker Alejandro Amenábar not only directed *The Others*, but also wrote the screenplay and composed the music for this ghostly tale in which two children suffer from severe photosensitivity. This is, in fact, a real disease known as Xeroderma Pigmentosum, which is extremely rare and for which there is no known cure. Even short exposure to the sun's ultraviolet rays can add up and prove lethal for sufferers of this disease.

NORMAN BATES: We all go a little mad sometimes. Haven't you?

PSYCHO
Dir. Alfred Hitchcock (1960)

FILM FACT: After *Psycho*, famous for its terrifying shower scene, hit the big screen, director Alfred Hitchcock received a letter from an aggrieved parent who explained that after seeing the movie *Les Diaboliques* his daughter refused to take a bath again and now, after seeing *Psycho*, was also refusing to shower. Hitchcock in his typical dry tone allegedly suggested that the man "send her to the dry cleaners."

MINA SEWARD: I heard dogs howling. And when the dream came, it seemed the whole room was filled with mist. It was so thick, I could just see the lamp by the bed, a tiny spark in the fog. And then I saw two red eyes staring at me, and a white livid face came down out of the mist. It came closer and closer. I felt its breath on my face and then its lips…

 ### DRACULA
Dir. Tod Browning (1931)

FILM FACT: The moment he opened his mouth and uttered those immortal words, "I am…Dra-cu-la. I bid you velcome…" Bela Lugosi became two things: the quintessential Dracula—often imitated, but never bettered, for years to come—and also typecast for his entire career. On screen his unforgettably intense look was aided by having tiny pinpricks of light shone into his eyes.

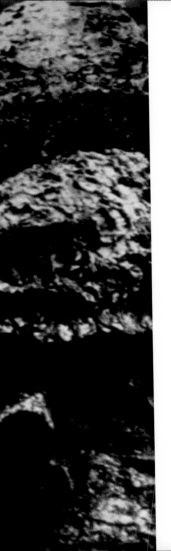

PAUL VON ESSEN: The conquest of new worlds always makes demands of human life. And there will always be men who will accept the risk.

FIRST MAN INTO SPACE
Dir. Robert Day (1959)

FILM FACT: The timing of *First Man into Space*—which was, despite the American cast and screenwriter, actually a British film—could not have been better. The launch of Sputnik was still fresh in the world's mind and everyone was gearing up for Soviet cosmonaut Yuri Gagarin to make his historic journey across the new frontier to become the real "first man into space."

PINHEAD: We will tear your soul apart.

 HELLRAISER
Dir. Clive Barker (1987)

FILM FACT: Actor Doug Bradley may have felt restricted by the mega six-hour sessions it took to get him into his full Pinhead makeup, but director Clive Barker was more than motivated by the constraints under which he had to work. He managed to turn the potentially disastrous situation of filming within the confines of an actual house into an example of fine cinematography and creativity, with shots that set new standards in filmmaking.

Feast your eyes! Glut your soul on my accursed ugliness!

Gaston Leroux

THE PHANTOM OF THE OPERA
Dir. Rupert Julian (1925)

FILM FACT: Lon Chaney was a master of disguise and he devised his own makeup for the Phantom. He plumped out his cheeks with cotton and glued his ears back, then he attached a rubber and wire device to his head under his bald cap and a strip of thin, translucent material to his nostrils to tilt his nose back. This is said to have caused him to suffer nosebleeds, but the effect proved worthwhile when several people were so shocked at the premiere, they fainted.

Who will survive and what will be left of them?

Tagline from the film

THE TEXAS CHAINSAW MASSACRE
Dir. Tobe Hooper (1974)

FILM FACT: Actor Edwin Neal, who played the Hitchhiker, is said to have described the endless hours spent filming the dinner scene for this movie as worse than his time spent serving in Vietnam. This may not seem quite so surprising when you consider that it was filmed over many hours during a heat wave in an airless room stuffed full of rotting dead animal carcasses and decomposing food.

SETH BRUNDLE: Uh, the computer got confused.... It mated us, me and the fly. We hadn't even been properly introduced.... Now I'm not Seth Brundle anymore. I'm the offspring of, um, Brundle and housefly.

THE FLY
Dir. David Cronenberg (1986)

FILM FACT: Director David Cronenberg wanted to steer clear of the 1958 film's choice of having a fly with a human's head and a human with a fly's head. Instead he sought to portray a literal fusion of a man and an insect that would look like an embodiment of the two. The result was grotesque makeup that took five hours to apply and the resulting "Brundlefly" is enough to make anyone's flesh creep.

He remembered that she was pretty, and, more, that she had a special grace in the intimacy of life. She had the secret of individuality which excites—and escapes.

Joseph Conrad

LA BELLE ET LA BÊTE (BEAUTY AND THE BEAST)
Dir. Jean Cocteau (1946)

FILM FACT: This classic tale remains stylish and contemporary today, possibly because many of the costumes were created under the guidance of fashion guru Pierre Cardin. Its enduring appeal may also be because there is a version of the movie that gives you the option to watch it along with the original opera score created by Philip Glass that is perfectly synchronized to the film.

QUINT: The thing about a shark, it's got lifeless eyes, black eyes, like a doll's eyes. When it comes at you it doesn't seem to be livin'...until he bites you, and those black eyes roll over white.

 JAWS
Dir. Steven Spielberg (1975)

FILM FACT: Fate played a vital part in the choices made during the filming of *Jaws*. The mechanical shark had a tendency to break down on a regular basis and Spielberg could not depend on it for any lengthy shots. So he decided to use the camera in a different way, filming much of the movie from the shark's perspective—in effect using the camera as the shark. This resulted in a compelling and often terrifying quality that may otherwise never have existed.

DR. FRANKENSTEIN: Look! It's moving. It's alive. It's alive…It's alive, it's moving, it's alive, it's alive, it's alive, it's alive, it's alive! Oh…in the name of God! Now I know what it feels like to be God!

FRANKENSTEIN
DIR. JOHN WHALE (1931)

FILM FACT: These infamous lines were found in their entirety in the original print of this film about Dr. Henry Frankenstein who creates a creature from body parts and brings it to life. However, the censors demanded the removal of the final phrase because it was considered blasphemous and the film went out with a loud crack of thunder drowning it out. Only recently was an original sound recording discovered which, with the help of modern technology, allowed the lines to be restored.

PENGUIN: I am an animal,
I am not a human being.

 BATMAN RETURNS
Dir. Tim Burton (1992)

FILM FACT: The twelve King penguins and twenty-four Black-foot penguins that appeared in this movie were treated even more luxuriously than their human co-stars. They were housed in two specially designed forty-foot trailers, which were temperature controlled and had their own swimming pools, and they were fed with fresh fish delivered daily from the docks.

JACK TORRANCE:
Danny! I'm coming!
You can't get away!
I'm right behind ya.

THE SHINING
Dir. Stanley Kubrick (1980)

FILM FACT: Compulsive director Stanley Kubrick was notorious for requesting countless retakes, but he got his shot of blood pouring through a set of elevator doors in just three takes. However, this was after a year of yelling, "It doesn't look like blood" at the special effects team when they presented him with various kinds of fake blood. He eventually got a blood substitute he was happy with, but then had to convince the censors that it was actually rusty water and not blood, so they would let him use the shot as the film's trailer.

JACK: On the moors, we were attacked by a lycanthrope, a werewolf. I was murdered, an unnatural death, and now I walk the earth in limbo until the werewolf's curse is lifted.
DAVID: Shut up!
JACK: The wolf's bloodline must be severed; the last remaining werewolf must be destroyed. It's you, David…

 ### AN AMERICAN WEREWOLF IN LONDON
Dir. John Landis (1981)

FILM FACT: Director John Landis witnessed a gypsy funeral in Yugoslavia while working on the movie *Kelly's Heroes* in 1970. The coffin had been draped with garlic, which he was told was to ensure the corpse did not return to haunt anyone. This gave him the idea to make a werewolf movie with a twist where a corpse does just that.

GOLLUM: They cursed us. Murderer they called us. They cursed us and drove us away... And we wept, Precious, didn't we? We wept to be so alone. And we only lust to catch fish so juicy sweet. And we forgot the taste of bread, the sound of trees, the softness of the wind. We even forgot our own name.

THE LORD OF THE RINGS: THE RETURN OF THE KING
Dir. Peter Jackson (2003)

FILM FACT: Although Gollum was created using computer-generated imagery (CGI), the role was entirely performed by actor Andy Serkis—the creature was then painted into the scene in his place. Serkis' tremendous performance drew calls for him to be nominated as Best Supporting Actor at the Academy Awards. However, despite Peter Jackson's compelling argument—"there was one person, an experienced, skilled actor, making all of the decisions on behalf of Gollum. [Andy] would decide how Gollum would move, how he would act, what emotion he would have"—Serkis was ruled as ineligible for an award because Gollum was a CGI character.

FREDDY KRUEGER: Not strong enough, yet. Well, I will be soon enough. Until then I'll let Jason have some fun.

 ### FREDDY VS. JASON
Dir. Ronny Yu (2003)

FILM FACT: Casting was a very serious issue for the filmmakers bringing together the legendary monsters from *A Nightmare on Elm Street* and *Friday the 13th* and it lead to a search for a new Jason. They needed an actor who was capable of towering above Robert Englund, who plays Freddy, but with eyes that could show pain, hurt, and despair. They eventually found their perfect Jason in stuntman Ken Kirzinger.

MACREADY: I don't know, it's like this: thousands of years ago this spaceship crashes, and this thing, whatever it is, jumps out or crawls out…

THE THING
Dir. John Carpenter (1982)

FILM FACT: Sometimes, in order to produce the right effect, filmmakers have to go to extremes—and, in this case, it was extreme temperatures. To create the perfect frozen Antarctic landscape for his isolated research base, prolific filmmaker John Carpenter had to get beyond a Los Angeles heat wave and refrigerate the film studios down to 40°F.

Prehistoric sea-giant rages against city!

Tagline from the film

THE BEAST FROM 20,000 FATHOMS
Dir. Eugène Lourié (1953)

FILM FACT: Apparently, while visiting the set of this movie about a monster that is accidentally thawed out by scientists in the Arctic and then goes on the rampage in New York, writer Ray Bradury was asked for his opinion on the script. After reading it, the writer mentioned that it appeared to be remarkably like a short story he had published in a newspaper several years before—and within hours he received a formal offer to buy the film rights!

The indestructible creature! Bloated with the blood of its victims!

Tagline from the film

 ## THE BLOB
Dir. Irvin S. Yeaworth Jr. (1958)

FILM FACT: This comic science-fiction movie was originally planned as a second feature on a double bill, but it proved so popular with the ticket-buying public—more people wanted to see *The Blob* than the movie that it was supporting—that it soon became a main feature. The monstrous Blob itself was manufactured using a small weather balloon and silicone gel, and it starred alongside a youthful Steven McQueen in his first lead role.

NIAL

MIDNIGHT SPOOK SHOW
DAUGHTER °F HORROR
ALSO BELA LUGOSI

DITIONED *Healthfully* AIR CONDITIONED

WATCH
REPAIRING

ARDETH BEY: Now, this creature is the bringer of death. He will never eat, he will never sleep, and he will never stop.

THE MUMMY
Dir. Stephen Sommers (1999)

FILM FACT: In contrast to the earlier versions of this tale, Stephen Sommers's take on *The Mummy* is packed with action, plenty of humor, and stunning special effects—including some rather feisty man-eating scarabs that will leave your flesh crawling for a long time to come. The film was immediately so successful that Sommers apparently said that the morning after it was released Universal Pictures telephoned him to say they needed another one fast!

See the armies of the world destroyed! See the birth of the world's most terrifying monster! See the war of the giants!

Tagline from the film

 ## MOSURA TAI GOJIRA (GODZILLA VS. MOTHRA)
Dir. Ishirô Honda (1964)

FILM FACT: When the American distributors of this classic Japanese monster movie were preparing *Mosura tai Gojira* for release in the US, they decided to shoot some extra scenes just for American audiences. They borrowed the famous Godzilla suit—known as the "Mosugoji" suit—that had been specially designed for the movie by Teizo Toshimitsu. Then they filmed several new scenes showing American troops attacking the giant reptilelike sea monster with missiles to add to the Americanized version of the film.

As soon as dawn appeared, fresh and rosy-fingered, the Cyclops re-lit the fire...he once more snatched up a couple of my men and prepared his meal.

Homer

THE 7TH VOYAGE OF SINBAD
Dir. Nathan Juran (1958)

FILM FACT: For this epic adventure film, world-renowned stop-motion animator Ray Harryhausen created one of his most memorable monsters—the rampaging Cyclops! His monster was capable of moving in and around the human actors (quite a feat in the days before modern computer technology), a technique which was another Harryhausen first and, as such, demanded a new name, "dynamation."

CARL DENHAM: He was a king and a god in the world he knew, but now he comes to civilization merely a captive—a show to gratify your curiosity. Ladies and gentlemen, look at Kong, the eighth wonder of the world.

 ## KING KONG
Dir. Merian C. Cooper (1933)

FILM FACT: The giant monster, King Kong, was represented by several metal and foam rubber models, measuring only eighteen inches high. One of the most peculiarly pleasing aspects of the famous ape is that its fur noticeably ripples up there on the big screen. This is due to a happy accident: each time a stop motion shot was taken of the creature and it was moved into position for the next frame, the animators simply forgot to brush its fur back into place.

LAURIE STRODE: I've been waiting for you Michael… I knew you'd come for me sooner or later. What took you so long?

HALLOWEEN: RESURRECTION
Rick Rosenthal (2002)

FILM FACT: Almost twenty-five years after John Carpenter directed the first *Halloween* movie, serial killer Michael Myers is back to his old tricks in this, the eighth movie in the popular horror franchise. Everyone who has seen one of these movies will remember the creepy mask always worn by the murderer, but not many people know that due to the severe budget constraints of the original movie the murderer's mask was actually a mask of actor William Shatner, better known as *Star Trek*'s Captain Kirk, which the crew altered simply by painting it white and reshaping the eyeholes.

Creature from a million years ago!
Every man his mortal enemy…and
a woman's beauty his prey!

Tagline from the film

 ## CREATURE FROM THE BLACK LAGOON
Dir. Jack Arnold (1954)

FILM FACT: When designing the costume for the prehistoric Amazon creature, or Gill-Man, the crew decided that there was no way to incorporate air tanks into the costume that couldn't be seen by the audience. So they hired professional swimmer Ricou Browning to play the monster when underwater because he could hold his breath for up to four minutes and wouldn't give away the fact that the creature wasn't, in fact, breathing through its gills.

DIANE: Sweetheart, do you remember last night when you woke up, and you said "They're here"?
CAROL ANNE: Uh huh…
DIANE: Well, who did you mean?
CAROL ANNE: The TV People.

POLTERGEIST
Dir. Tobe Hooper (1982)

FILM FACT: This film is a tribute to the filmmakers' inventiveness and talent for bricolage, with their low-cost special effects including chairs being dragged along by wires, steak puppetry, and an entire house being sucked into the ground! For this final scene, a model house was painstakingly wired and prepared so that, at just the right moment, it was blasted from above whilst being pulled by its wires and sucked downwards by a vacuum. The resulting spectacular effect so impressed Steven Spielberg that he is said to have the remnants of the model mounted and displayed on his piano.

DR. ALEZIAS: The demon wolf is not evil, unless the man he has bitten is evil. And it feels good to be a wolf, doesn't it?

 WOLF
Dir. Mike Nichols (1994)

FILM FACT: At a dinner for director Mike Nichols, Meryl Streep told a story about an incident that happened on the set of *Wolf*. Nichols apparently crumpled up with severe chest pains and Jack Nicholson rushed to his side, caring for him until the doctor arrived. The doctor pushed Nicholson aside, demanding to know who he was, and Jack, in full werewolf makeup and with a deadpan expression on his face, said, "His son..."—making Mike Nichols burst out laughing.

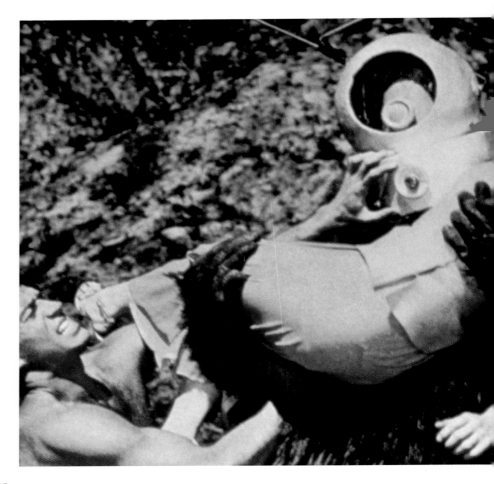

Moon monsters launch attack against Earth! How can science meet the menace of astral assassins?

Tagline from the film

 ## ROBOT MONSTER
Dir. Phil Tucker (1953)

FILM FACT: This 1950s B movie has all the classic traits that make these films so much fun, from the low-rate special effects to the cheesy dialogue and awful plot. The invading alien monster was supposed to be played by a man in a typical tin robot suit, but the filmmakers couldn't afford to hire one. Instead they cast George Barrows to play the monster because he already owned his own gorilla suit and they simply put a traditional diving helmet with an antenna stuck on top on his head.

AGENT J: Worms! Give me some cover fire!
WORM: Too scared, can't move!

MEN IN BLACK II
Barry Sonnenfeld (2002)

FILM FACT: The coffee-guzzling "Worm Guys" proved to be so popular in the first *Men in Black* movie that director Barry Sonnenfeld made sure they had a much bigger role in this sequel: "I loved those guys because they were so politically incorrect; they smoked cigarettes, they took long work breaks and they were obnoxious. So, they're back."

COACH DRIVER: They are not men, Monsieur. They are dead bodies—zombies! The living dead! Corpses taken from their graves and made to work in the sugar mills and fields at night.

WHITE ZOMBIE
Dir. Victor Halperin (1932)

FILM FACT: This haunting, but often forgotten, monster movie from the Halperin Brothers is considered to be the first ever zombie movie. It is also one of the great Bela Lugosi's first films, but it is said that he wouldn't watch the film himself because he was paid very little for his role as a sinister hypnotist and voodoo master, while the Halperin brothers profited far more from the film's success.

On mounting a rising ground, which brought the figure of his fellow-traveller in relief against the sky, gigantic in height, and muffled in a cloak, Ichabod was horror-struck, on perceiving that he was headless!—but his horror was still more increased, on observing that the head, which should have rested on his shoulders, was carried before him on the pommel of the saddle.

Washington Irving

 ## Sleepy Hollow
Dir. Tim Burton (1999)

FILM FACT: There is a heartfelt and charming tribute to Disney in this wonderfully scary movie. In one scene, Constable Ichabod Crane crosses a covered bridge and hears the frogs underneath it croaking "Ichabod" and "Headless Horseman." This is exactly what happened in Disney's 1959 animated film *The Legend of Sleepy Hollow*, which director Tim Burton admits influenced him when he was making his version.

Picture credits

Everett Collection/Rex Features: pages 3, 8, 12, 17, 19, 20, 27, 32, 35, 41, 42, 47, 49, 57, 60, 65, 66, 73, 74, 81, 85, 87.
SIPA Press/Rex Features: page 7.
Snap Photo Library/Rex Features: pages 15, 24, 28, 37, 39, 44, 53, 54, 58, 68, 70, 82, 88, 90, 93, 97, 101, 102, 106.
© 20th Century Fox/Everett Collection/Rex Features: pages 11, 31, 63.
© Columbia/Everett Collection/Rex Features: pages 23, 104.
© New Line/Everett Collection/Rex Features: pages 77, 78.
© MGM/Everett Collection/Rex Features: page 98.
© Miramax/Everett Collection/Rex Features: page 94.
© Paramount/Everett Collection/Rex Features: page 109.
© Paramount/The Kobal Collection: page 50.

Text credits

p.6: Dialogue from *Mars Attacks!* (Warner Bros; screenwriter Jonathan Gems). p.9: Dialogue from *Hunchback of Notre Dame* (RKO Radio Pictures; screenwriters Bruno Frank and Sonya Levien). p.10: Tagline from *Alien* (20th Century Fox/ Brandywine Productions). p.13: Dialogue from *The Mummy* (Universal Pictures; screenwriter John L. Balderston). p.14: Dialogue from *Batman* (Guber-Peters Company/PolyGram/Warner Bros; screenwriters Sam Hamm and Warren Skaaren). p.17: Tagline from *Bride of Frankenstein* (Universal Pictures). p.21: Dialogue from *The Wizard of Oz* (Loew's Inc/MGM; screenwriters Noel Langley, Florence Ryerson, and Edgar Allan Woolf). p.22: Dialogue from *Misery* (Castle Rock/Nelson Entertainment; screenwriter William Goldman). p.25: Tagline from *Jason and the Argonauts* (Columbia Pictures/ Morningside Worldwide). p.26: Dialogue from *The Birds* (Alfred J. Hitchcock Productions/Universal Pictures; screenwriter Evan Hunter). p.29: Dialogue from *The Invisible Man* (Universal Pictures; screenwriter R. C. Sheriff). p.33: Tagline from *The War of the Worlds* (Paramount Pictures). p.34: Dialogue from *Blade Runner* (Blade Runner Partnership/ The Ladd Company; screenwriters Hampton Fancher and David Peoples). p.36: Dialogue from *The Wolf Man* (Universal Pictures; screenwriter Curt Siodmak). p.39: Dialogue from *Invasion of the Saucer Men* (Malibu Productions; Robert J. Gurney Jr. and Al Martin). p.43: Tagline from *Gremlins 2: The New Batch* (Amblin Entertainment/Warner Bros). p.45: Tagline from *Dr. Jekyll and Mr. Hyde* (Paramount Pictures). p.46: Dialogue from *Cape Fear* (Amblin Entertainment/Cappa Films/Tribeca Productions/Universal Pictures; screenwriters James R. Webb and Wesley Strick). p.48: Dialogue from *The Others* (Cruise/ Wagner Productions/Las Producciones del Escorpión/Sociedad General de Cine; screenwriter Alejandro Amenábar). p.51:

Dialogue from *Psycho* (Shamley Productions/Paramount Pictures; screenwriter Joseph Stefano). p.52: Dialogue from *Dracula* (Universal Pictures; screenwriters Hamilton Deane, John L. Balderston, and Garrett Fort).p.55: Dialogue from *First Man into Space* (Amalgamated Productions; screenwriter John Croydon). p.56: Dialogue from *Hellraiser* (Cinemarque Entertainment/Film Futures/Rivdel Films; screenwriter Clive Barker). p.60: Tagline from *The Texas Chainsaw Massacre* (Vortex). p.63: Dialogue from *The Fly* (Brooksfilms; screenwriters David Cronenberg, George Langelaan, and Charles Edward Pogue). p.67: Dialogue from *Jaws* (Universal Pictures/Zanuck/Brown Productions; screenwriters Peter Benchley and Carl Gorrlieb). p.68: Dialogue from *Frankenstein* (Universal Pictures; screenwriters John L. Balderston, Francis Edward Faragoh, and Garrett Fort). p.71: Dialogue from *Batman Returns* (Polygram Pictures/ Warner Bros; screenwriter Daniel Waters). p.72: Dialogue from *The Shining* (Hawk Films/Peregrine/Producers Circle/ Warner Bros; screenwriters Stanley Kubrick and Diane Johnson). p.75: Dialogue from *An American Werewolf in London* (American Werewolf Inc/Guber-Peters Company/Lyncanthrope/PolyGram; screenwriter John Landis). p.76: Dialogue from *The Lord of the Rings: The Return of the King* (New Line Cinema/WingNut Films/Lord Dritte Productions/The Saul Zaentz Company; screenwriter Fran Walsh, Philippa Boyens, and Peter Jackson). p.79: Dialogue from *Freddy vs. Jason* (New Line Cinema; screenwriters Damian Shannon and Mark Swift). p.80: Dialogue from *The Thing* (Turman-Foster Company/Universal Pictures; screenwriter Bill Lancaster). p.83: Tagline from *The Beast from 20,000 Fathoms* (Mutual Pictures of California). p.84: Tagline from *The Blob* (Fairview Productions/Tonylyn Productions). p.87: Dialogue from *The Mummy* (Alphaville Films/Universal Pictures; screenwriters Lloyd Fonvielle, Kevin Jarre, and Stephen Sommers). p.88: Tagline from *Mosura tai Gojira* (Toho/American International Pictures). p.93: Dialogue from *King Kong* (RKO Radio Pictures; screenwriters Merian C. Cooper, Edgar Wallace, James Ashmore Creelman, and Ruth Rose). p.95: Dialogue from *Halloween: Resurrection* (Dimension Films/Nightfall Productions/Trancas International Films Inc; screenwriters Larry Brand and Sean Hood). p.96: Tagline from *Creature from the Black Lagoon* (Universal International Pictures). p.99: Dialogue from *Poltergeist* (MGM; screenwriters Steven Spielberg, Michael Grais, and Mark Victor). p.100: Dialogue from *Wolf* (Columbia Pictures; screenwriters Jim Harrison and Wesley Strick). p.103: Tagline from *Robot Monster* (Three Dimensional Pictures). p.104: Dialogue from *Men in Black II* (Amblin Entertainment/Columbia Pictures/MacDonald/Parkes Productions; screenwriters Robert Gordon and Barry Fanaro). p.107: Dialogue from *White Zombie* (Edward Halperin Productions/ Victor Halperin Productions; screenwriter Garnett Weston).

We would like to thank the creators both before and behind the camera, who have educated, informed, and entertained us all, especially the many talented screenwriters whose words have enriched this book. To them we are indebted. We apologize for any unintentional error or omission in the acknowledgments above and would be pleased to hear from any companies or individuals who may have been accidentally overlooked.

Published by MQ Publications Limited

12 The Ivories, 6–8 Northampton Street, London, N1 2HY

Tel: +44 (0)20 7359 2244 / Fax: +44 (0)20 7359 1616

Email: mail@mqpublications.com

Website: www.mqpublications.com

ISBN: 1-84072-972-4

1 3 5 7 9 0 8 6 4 2

Printed and bound in Singapore